I CAN'T SAY THAT!

PARENT

WORKBOOK

COREY GILBERT, PHD, LPC

I CAN'T SAY THAT!

PARENT

WORKBOOK

GOING BEYOND
"THE TALK":
EQUIPPING YOUR CHILDREN
TO MAKE CHOICES ABOUT
SEXUALITY AND GENDER
FROM A BIBLICAL SEXUAL ETHIC

I Can't Say That! PARENT WORKBOOK

Going Beyond "The Talk": Equipping Your Children to Make Choices About Sexuality and Gender From a Biblical Sexual Ethic

Published by Rebel Press
Austin, TX
www.RebelPress.com

ISBN: 978-1-64339-865-5

Printed in the United States of America

I am so glad you decided to get this workbook to accompany my book. This workbook is meant to be a place for you to expand your knowledge and make a plan to serve and lead your family with confidence.

Go through the book and the questions posed here to help expand and solidify parts of your ETHOS — specifically building a **Biblical Sexual Ethic.**

Gain confidence. Gain strategy. This is only a start. The micro-conversations will still need to happen. You have a lot of hard work to do. But with this tool and the provided resources, and with a foundation in God's Word, you can do this. With community, even more so. Bless you and your journey to address hard conversations from a **biblical worldview.**

I am honored to go on this journey with you through this process.

Access more resources including video trainings and more content for free at:

http://parentbook.healinglives.com

Dr. G

I CAN'T SAY THAT!

THAT!

PARENT
WORKBOOK

CHAPTER 1

YOUR STORY: TAKING INVENTORY

What are topics you feel uncomfortable or unprepared to talk to your children about — list these here (it is important to get this in writing so you can better prepare and plan — and learn)?

_____

_____

_____

_____

_____

_____

_____

_____

_____

_____

Do you have fears for your children in any particular areas related to sexuality and relationships?

_____

_____

_____

_____

_____

_____

What are some questions you have today? Write these down — get them out of your head and onto paper.

_____

_____

_____

_____

_____

Read Deuteronomy 6:6–7

"And you must commit yourselves wholeheartedly to these commands that I am giving you today. Repeat them again and again to your children. Talk about them when you are at home and when you are on the road, when you are going to bed and when you are getting up" (NLT).

What does this passage tell you to do?

_____

_____

_____

_____

List opportunities that might arise throughout the week with your child (or children) to talk about a Biblical Sexual Ethic. Strategize here.

_____

_____

_____

_____

_____

_____

_____

_____

_____

_____

_____

_____

CHAPTER 2

STOP THE CHAIN OF IGNORANCE

You Are Not Alone

Read Titus 2:3–5

"Similarly, teach the older women to live in a way that honors God. They must not slander others or be heavy drinkers. Instead, they should teach others what is good. These older women must train the younger women to love their husbands and their children, to live wisely and be pure, to work in their homes, to do good, and to be submissive to their husbands. Then they will not bring shame on the word of God" (NLT).

Reword this passage as a command to yourself.

_____

_____

_____

_____

_____

_____

_____

How would you define "success" for your child as an adult?

_____

_____

_____

_____

_____

_____

What would a "Champion for Christ" look like as a teen or adult?

_____

_____

_____

_____

_____

_____

How would you define the difference between "protection" and "preparation?"

_____

_____

_____

_____

_____

_____

Are there any areas where you are solely protecting your children?

_____

_____

_____

_____

_____

_____

_____

_____

_____

How can you be more intentional at preparing them?

_____

_____

_____

_____

_____

_____

Are you silent on these topics? Are you waiting for them to come to you if they have questions?

_____

_____

_____

_____

_____

_____

_____

Begin a growing list of topics you want to be intentional about having micro-conversations with your children about. Break the silence!

_____

_____

_____

_____

_____

_____

_____

_____

_____

_____

How would you define micro-conversations?

_____

_____

_____

_____

_____

_____

_____

_____

_____

_____

The Change Begins With You

Read **Romans 12:2**

"Do not conform to the pattern of this world, but be transformed by the renewing of your mind" (NIV).

What do you think about most?

How are you continually renewing your mind?

_____

_____

_____

_____

_____

_____

_____

_____

_____

_____

_____

_____

_____

_____

Use the following space (and perhaps another notebook or Word document) to write out your sexual autobiography. This a detailed chronological account of your story and how you learned about sexuality, your growing knowledge, and your experiences.

_____

_____

_____

_____

_____

_____

_____

_____

_____

_____

_____

_____

_____

_____

_____

_____

_____

_____

_____

_____

_____

_____

_____

_____

_____

_____

Write specific beliefs you hold about sexuality that may need to be re-examined from a Biblical perspective.

_____

_____

_____

_____

_____

_____

_____

Write in one or two sentences what you believe about sexuality.

_____

_____

_____

_____

_____

Locate Scripture passages that support your view?

_____

_____

_____

_____

_____

_____

_____

_____

_____

_____

_____

Read **Galatians 2:20**

My old self has been crucified with Christ. It is no longer I who live, but Christ lives in me. So I live in this earthly body by trusting in the Son of God, who loved me and gave himself for me (NLT).

This passage teaches us that you can develop your spirit through choices you make in your mind and led by the Holy Spirit — what are these?

_____

_____

_____

_____

_____

_____

_____

_____

A reminder: **1 Peter 3:15**

"... always be ready to give a defense ..." (NLT)

Are you? Are you ready to do so? Are you prudent, sensible, discreet and compassionate?

_____

_____

_____

_____

_____

_____

_____

Where Are You Going?

If nothing changes in your household, what will your children believe about God, sexuality, and sexual behaviors (by learning from what you say and do)?

_____

_____

_____

_____

_____

_____

_____

What would you like your children to believe as adults?

_____

_____

_____

_____

_____

_____

_____

_____

_____

_____

_____

_____

_____

Read **Proverbs 14:15**

Only simpletons believe everything they're told! The prudent carefully consider their steps (NLT).

What steps do you need to take to ensure that your children end up where you would like them to be from the previous question?

_____

_____

_____

_____

_____

_____

_____

_____

_____

_____

You Can Teach An Old Dog New Tricks

As you think about the neuroplasticity of the brain and epigenetics, does this encourage you?

_____

_____

_____

_____

_____

Where would you like to experience change in your life?

_____

_____

_____

_____

_____

Read **Deuteronomy 30:19**

"Today I have given you the choice between life and death, between blessings and curses. Now I call on heaven and earth to witness the choice you make. Oh, that you would choose life, so that you and your descendants might live!" (NLT)

Do you choose life? This decision impacts generations.

_____

_____

_____

_____

The Student Has Become The Teacher

Do you believe the Bible's instructions on sexuality are to be followed and obeyed today?

_____

_____

_____

_____

Can you live by **2 Timonthy 1:7** — NOT having a spirit of fear and timidity?

For God has not given us a spirit of fear and timidity, but of power, love, and self-discipline (NLT).

_____

_____

_____

_____

Yes, I commit to leading my family, my children, and myself in a Biblical Sexual Ethic. I commit to reading, learning, and intentionally having micro-conversations.

Yes   No (I will defer this to others)   Maybe (define)

Read **2 Timothy 1:7** (see above) and

1 Corinthians 2:16

For, "Who can know the Lord's thoughts? Who knows enough to teach him?" But we understand these things, for we have the mind of Christ (NLT).

These passages are great reminders of our identity. What does it mean to be a parent that leads with power, love, and self-discipline? What does it mean to have the mind of Christ?

_____

_____

_____

_____

_____

Proverbs 22:6 reads:

Train up a child in the way he should go, And when he is old he will not depart from it (NKJV).

Commit to this incredible task - reword this verse and personalize it.

_____

_____

_____

_____

_____

_____

_____

_____

How do you reconcile **Proverbs 22:6** with people you know that walked away from their faith despite being "trained in the way they should go?"

_____

_____

_____

_____

_____

_____

_____

_____

CHAPTER 3

SEX ED FOR PARENTS

A Theology Of Sex

How would you define the difference between "preserving innocence" and "preventing ignorance"?

_____

_____

_____

_____

_____

_____

_____

_____

_____

_____

Is it possible for a parent to do both? How could you do this in your family?

_____

_____

_____

_____

_____

_____

Is being "in love" all that is necessary to begin a sexual relationship?

_____

_____

_____

_____

_____

_____

_____

Do you believe your children ARE or ARE NOT ready for a sexual relationship? Do your children believe they are?

_____

_____

_____

_____

_____

_____

_____

What if they are a hopeless romantic?
How can you disciple and encourage your
child if they are a hopeless romantic?

_____

_____

_____

Statistics guestimate that seventy percent of American
teens have already had sex. What can you do with
that information as a parent? If you have a teen, have
you asked them what their experiences have been
with their boyfriend/girlfriend if they one? Are you just
naively assuming, "not my child?"

_____

_____

_____

_____

_____

_____

Do you treat your sexuality with a sense of respect
and responsibility, or do you treat your sexuality with
disdain due to your own experiences? If your answer
is disdain, to what experience in your personal history
has led to this attitude toward sex and sexuality?

_____

_____

_____

_____

_____

When many of us were kids, if we had questions about sex, we looked at encyclopedias, National Geographic or Playboy magazines. Where do kids turn today?

_____

_____

_____

_____

_____

Parents, what was your sex education like? Was it a one-time conversation that was more lecture than a dialogue? Were your parents embarrassed? Was it left to the school or Church? What were your first glimpses of nudity and/or pornography? Was it in a print magazine?

_____

_____

_____

_____

_____

_____

How can we worship God with our bodies - specifically with our sexuality?

_____

_____

_____

_____

_____

_____

_____

Define chastity.

_____
_____
_____
_____
_____

Read **1 Thessalonians 4:3–8**

God's will is for you to be holy, so stay away from all sexual sin. Then each of you will control his own body and live in holiness and honor — not in lustful passion like the pagans who do not know God and his ways. Never harm or cheat a fellow believer in this matter by violating his wife, for the Lord avenges all such sins, as we have solemnly warned you before. God has called us to live holy lives, not impure lives. Therefore, anyone who refuses to live by these rules is not disobeying human teaching but is rejecting God, who gives his Holy Spirit to you (NLT).

What is God's desire for you and your children?

_____
_____
_____
_____
_____
_____
_____
_____
_____

Read **Titus 2:1–8**

As for you, Titus, promote the kind of living that reflects wholesome teaching. Teach the older men to exercise self-control, to be worthy of respect, and to live wisely. They must have sound faith and be filled with love and patience.

Similarly, teach the older women to live in a way that honors God. They must not slander others or be heavy drinkers. Instead, they should teach others what is good. These older women must train the younger women to love their husbands and their children, to live wisely and be pure, to work in their homes, to do good, and to be submissive to their husbands. Then they will not bring shame on the word of God.

In the same way, encourage the young men to live wisely. And you yourself must be an example to them by doing good works of every kind. Let everything you do reflect the integrity and seriousness of your teaching. Teach the truth so that your teaching can't be criticized. Then those who oppose us will be ashamed and have nothing bad to say about us (NLT).

Verses 11-14:

For the grace of God has been revealed, bringing salvation to all people. And we are instructed to turn from godless living and sinful pleasures. We should live in this evil world with wisdom, righteousness, and devotion to God, while we look forward with hope to that wonderful day when the glory of our great God and Savior, Jesus Christ, will be revealed. He gave his life to free us from every kind of sin, to cleanse us, and to make us his very own people, totally committed to doing good deeds (NLT).

What does this passage require of you?

_____

_____

_____

_____

_____

_____

Read **Ecclesiastes 7:16–18**

So don't be too good or too wise! Why destroy yourself? On the other hand, don't be too wicked either. Don't be a fool! Why die before your time? Pay attention to these instructions, for anyone who fears God will avoid both extremes (NLT).

Explain this passage.

_____

_____

_____

_____

_____

_____

_____

_____

_____

Read **Romans 12:1**

And so, dear brothers and sisters, I plead with you to give your bodies to God because of all he has done for you. Let them be a living and holy sacrifice—the kind he will find acceptable. This is truly the way to worship him (NLT).

What does it mean to offer our bodies as living sacrifices?

_____

_____

_____

_____

_____

_____

_____

Read **1 John 4:12b**

...if we love each other, God lives in us, and his love is brought to full expression in us (NLT).

This passage says that the evidence that God lives in us is declared by what action? How would you define "love"?

_____

_____

_____

_____

_____

_____

Read **Song of Solomon 5:16**

His mouth is sweetness itself; he is desirable in every way. Such, O women of Jerusalem, is my lover, my friend (NLT).

and **Proverbs 5:15**

Drink water from your own well— share your love only with your wife (NLT).

Explain these verses.

_____

_____

_____

_____

_____

_____

Read **1 Peter 5:8**

Stay alert! Watch out for your great enemy, the devil. He prowls around like a roaring lion, looking for someone to devour (NLT).

Who is watching and seeking to destroy you?

_____

_____

_____

_____

_____

_____

_____

Read **Song of Solomon 7**. Take notes on these verses. What stands out? Do you have any questions? Thoughts?

How beautiful are your sandaled feet, O queenly maiden.

Your rounded thighs are like jewels, the work of a skilled craftsman.

Your navel is perfectly formed like a goblet filled with mixed wine.

Between your thighs lies a mound of wheat bordered with lilies.

Your breasts are like two fawns, twin fawns of a gazelle.

Your neck is as beautiful as an ivory tower.

Your eyes are like the sparkling pools in Heshbon by the gate of Bath-rabbim.

Your nose is as fine as the tower of Lebanon overlooking Damascus.

Your head is as majestic as Mount Carmel, and the sheen of your hair radiates royalty.

The king is held captive by its tresses.

Oh, how beautiful you are! How pleasing, my love, how full of delights!

You are slender like a palm tree, and your breasts are like its clusters of fruit.

I said, "I will climb the palm tree and take hold of its fruit." May your breasts be like grape clusters, and the fragrance of your breath like apples.

May your kisses be as exciting as the best wine—

Young Woman

Yes, wine that goes down smoothly for my lover, flowing gently over lips and teeth.

I am my lover's, and he claims me as his own.

Come, my love, let us go out to the fields and spend the night among the wildflowers.

Let us get up early and go to the vineyards to see if the grapevines have budded, if the blossoms have opened, and if the pomegranates have bloomed. There I will give you my love.

There the mandrakes give off their fragrance, and the finest fruits are at our door, new delights as well as old, which I have saved for you, my lover (NLT).

_____

_____

_____

_____

_____

_____

_____

_____

_____

Your Story

As you remember and refelct do not rush this — it is the foundation of what's to come.

How did you think about love and sex when you were a teenager?

_____

_____

_____

_____

_____

_____

_____

_____

What were the messages you received from your parents, your church, school, teachers, friends, media, etc?

_____

_____

_____

_____

_____

_____

_____

_____

_____

_____

_____

What was bad touch? What was acceptable? What was deemed horrible or sinful? What was sick or disgusting or gross?

_____

_____

_____

_____

_____

_____

What was beautiful, permissible, taught well, with boundaries, given clear healthy guidelines, discussed openly with age-appropriate tact?

_____

_____

_____

_____

_____

_____

Have you been impacted by trauma? If so, it most likely has impacted your relationships, view of self, and how you think and talk about sex and sexuality.

_____

_____

_____

_____

_____

_____

A *Theology* Of Marriage

How was marriage defined in your church, community, or school when you were growing up?

_____

_____

_____

_____

_____

_____

What ideas did you have about marriage based on your family?

_____

_____

_____

_____

_____

_____

How did your parents deal with "IT"?

_____

_____

_____

_____

_____

_____

_____

What impact have the following had on your ETHOS as you developed a worldview on marriage and sex within marriage?

- Your personal experience (good and bad)

_____

_____

_____

_____

_____

- Family history (historical, cultural, tradition)

_____

_____

_____

_____

_____

- The lack of conversation–the problem of silence

_____

_____

_____

_____

_____

- Biblical precedent (and/or interpretation)

_____

_____

_____

_____

_____

Read **Genesis 1:26**

Then God said, "Let us make human beings in our image, to be like us. They will reign over the fish in the sea, the birds in the sky, the livestock, all the wild animals on the earth, and the small animals that scurry along the ground." (NLT)

What does it mean to be made in His "likeness?"

_____

_____

_____

_____

_____

_____

Read **Leviticus 20:7**

So set yourselves apart to be holy, for I am the Lord your God (NLT).

What does it mean to set yourself apart?

_____

_____

_____

_____

_____

_____

_____

_____

_____

What are the two vehicles God has given us within which to live out being ONE?

1. _____
   _____
   _____

2. _____
   _____
   _____

What lessons did you learn about sex and your sexuality growing up?

_____
_____
_____
_____
_____

What lessons were you taught from your church?

_____
_____
_____
_____
_____

Have you had the experience of a bad relationship that crossed the lines? How do you think it has impacted you?

_____
_____
_____
_____

Have you processed the hurt and loss from abuse you endured? The effect of abuse can be felt years later.

_____

_____

_____

_____

_____

What are the 3 "P's"? How important do you think each of these are?

_____

_____

_____

_____

_____

_____

_____

If you are divorced or have a blended family, write out some of your challenges.

_____

_____

_____

_____

_____

_____

_____

What are questions you have?

_____

_____

_____

_____

_____

_____

_____

_____

_____

_____

_____

What are some of your most difficult moments that need your attention and intention?

_____

_____

_____

_____

_____

_____

_____

_____

_____

_____

_____

_____

_____

_____

Love, Sex, And Neuroscience

Oxytocin is our _____ chemical. What else does it do?

_____

_____

_____

_____

_____

Cortisol is what kind of hormone?

_____

_____

_____

_____

_____

What is the antibody IgA?

_____

_____

_____

_____

_____

What is the role of dopamine in attraction, pleasure and reward?

_____

_____

_____

_____

_____

The prefrontal cortex (PFC) is involved in:

_____

_____

_____

_____

The anterior cingulate gyrus (ACG)—when healthy—helps us:

_____

_____

_____

_____

The deep limbic system (DLS) is intimately involved in our:

_____

_____

_____

_____

The basal ganglia (BG) is involved in integrating:

_____

_____

_____

_____

Temporal lobes (TLs) help with:

_____

_____

_____

_____

Does this section help you see the complexities and the beauty of God's perfect design in how we are created? What are some potential problems that can arise - both medically and emotionally?

_____

_____

_____

_____

_____

_____

_____

_____

Read **Matthew 19:5–6**

And he said, "'This explains why a man leaves his father and mother and is joined to his wife, and the two are united into one.' Since they are no longer two but one, let no one split apart what God has joined together." (NLT)

Explain the design for marriage based off this passage.

_____

_____

_____

_____

_____

_____

_____

_____

_____

Anatomy

Describe the basic male anatomy as you would to your son or daughter at ages five, ten, and fifteen. What is the difference in your description?

_____

_____

_____

_____

_____

_____

_____

_____

_____

Describe the basic female anatomy as you would to your son or daughter at ages five, ten, and fifteen. What is the difference in your description?

_____

_____

_____

_____

_____

_____

_____

_____

Describe the basic "coming together" of the anatomy of men and women as you would to your son or daughter at ages five, ten, and fifteen. What is the difference? Why is it different?

_____

_____

_____

_____

_____

_____

_____

_____

_____

_____

_____

_____

_____

_____

_____

CHAPTER 4

TALKING TO YOUR KIDS

Birth To Age Five

Look for opportunities to have micro-conversations with your child over the next few days about some or all of the following topics: nudity, boundaries, pornography, boyfriends/girlfriends, marriage, anatomy, and attraction. How did the conversation come up? Did they have any questions?

_____

_____

_____

_____

_____

_____

_____

What are your children absorbing from your family at this age? Explain.

_____

_____

_____

_____

_____

_____

_____

Someone will have an explicit conversation with them. Who do you want to be the first person to address these topics with your child?

_____

_____

_____

_____

_____

_____

_____

When should you start having *micro-conversations* with your child(ren) on issues surrounding sexuality?

_____

_____

_____

_____

_____

_____

List topics you want to intentionally address with your children at this age.

_____

_____

_____

_____

_____

_____

_____

_____

_____

Where do you want your child to go in terms of their sexual ethic — their ETHOS? Read **Proverbs 22:6:**

Train up a child in the way he should go, And when he is old he will not depart from it (NKJV).

_____

_____

_____

_____

_____

_____

_____

_____

_____

_____

Kinder To Elementary Age (6~10)

Is your son prepared to face his first exposure to a naked picture on a screen? What about a video? Is your daughter ready to see those images as she processes where she is at in comparison?

_____

_____

_____

_____

_____

_____

_____

Ask your son or daughter if they have seen naked pictures or videos. Did they think anything was confusing or do they have any questions about what they saw?

_____

_____

_____

_____

_____

_____

_____

_____

_____

Explain the difference between "the talk" and micro-conversations.

_____

_____

_____

_____

_____

_____

_____

What is your ETHOS for dating, opposite-sex relationships, the "M" word, and pornography?

_____

_____

_____

_____

_____

_____

_____

How can you be careful and sensitive to the navigation of sexual identity which can be a struggle for some youth.

_____

_____

_____

_____

_____

List topics you want to intentionally address with your children at this age.

_____

_____

_____

_____

_____

_____

_____

_____

_____

_____

_____

Middle School To High School (11~17)

What tends to take up the most of your time as an adult? How do you spend your free time?

_____

_____

_____

_____

_____

_____

_____

_____

_____

How would you describe the husband or wife that you want your child to be one day?

_____

_____

_____

_____

_____

_____

_____

_____

How would you describe the husband or wife that you want for your child one day?

_____

_____

_____

_____

_____

_____

_____

What is important to you in the raising of a son and his masculinity?

_____

_____

_____

_____

_____

_____

_____

What is important to you in the raising of a daughter and her femininity?

_____

_____

_____

_____

_____

_____

_____

_____

How can you model discipline, wisdom, and integrity in your interactions through social media?

_____

_____

_____

_____

_____

_____

_____

What rules are important to you as a parent?

_____

_____

_____

_____

_____

_____

_____

What are your goals in having these rules (stewardship)?

_____

_____

_____

_____

_____

_____

Do you want your son or daughter to be a leader that helps others make wise decisions, and overcome past choices and traumas? How can they encourage others to lead a life that honors the God of the Bible?

_____

_____

_____

_____

_____

_____

_____

List topics you want to intentionally address with your children at this age.

_____

_____

_____

_____

_____

_____

CHAPTER 5

QUESTIONS ABOUT GENDER, HOMOSEXUALITY, AND SAME-SEX ATTRACTION

Gender Questions

What is your current theology and understanding of the beauty and intricacies of male and female, masculinity and femininity, of gender? Is it a simple binary belief and or is there more to it?

_____

_____

_____

_____

_____

_____

_____

_____

_____

_____

_____

_____

_____

Define masculinity.

_____

_____

_____

_____

_____

_____

_____

_____

Define femininity.

_____

_____

_____

_____

_____

_____

_____

_____

_____

What are your son and daughter being taught about masculinity in your home?

_____

_____

_____

_____

_____

_____

What are your son and daughter being taught about femininity in your home?

_____

_____

_____

_____

_____

_____

How can you prepare your child to date well?

_____

_____

_____

_____

_____

_____

_____

_____

How can you prepare your son or daughter to
be respectful of others' bodies and privacy?

_____

_____

_____

_____

_____

_____

How can you prepare them to have respect for their
body and not to expose it or use it as a tool or weapon?

_____

_____

_____

_____

_____

_____

How can you help them use their masculinity or
femininity to serve others? Brainstorm ideas here.

_____

_____

_____

_____

_____

_____

God created us as two distinct genders. Why do you think God did this (**Genesis 1:27**)?

So God created human beings in his own image. In the image of God he created them; male and female he created them (NLT).

_____

_____

_____

_____

_____

_____

_____

_____

_____

Read **Genesis 2:18–25**

Then the Lord God said, "It is not good for the man to be alone. I will make a helper who is just right for him." So the Lord God formed from the ground all the wild animals and all the birds of the sky. He brought them to the man to see what he would call them, and the man chose a name for each one. He gave names to all the livestock, all the birds of the sky, and all the wild animals. But still there was no helper just right for him.

So the Lord God caused the man to fall into a deep sleep. While the man slept, the Lord God took out one of the man's ribs and closed up the opening. Then the Lord God made a woman from the rib, and he brought her to the man.

"At last!" the man exclaimed.

"This one is bone from my bone,

and flesh from my flesh!

She will be called 'woman,'

because she was taken from 'man.'"

This explains why a man leaves his father and mother and is joined to his wife, and the two are united into one.

Now the man and his wife were both naked, but they felt no shame (NLT).

This passage takes gender further with His design for marriage and children. Brainstorm your own ideas as to "why."

_____

_____

_____

_____

_____

_____

_____

_____

_____

_____

_____

_____

_____

Homosexuality

What is important to you to teach and lead your children in a biblical understanding of homosexuality?

_____

_____

_____

_____

_____

_____

_____

_____

_____

What questions could you ask your children to help shape them and guide them intentionally?

_____

_____

_____

_____

_____

_____

_____

_____

_____

_____

_____

_____

_____

Do you need to soften or enter into conversations more carefully with your children so that they won't shut down, but will instead share what is going on in their hearts and lives?

_____

_____

_____

_____

_____

_____

_____

Write out some talking points you would use to discuss homosexuality from a biblical perspective.

_____

_____

_____

_____

_____

_____

_____

Write down some questions you have and email those to me at **questions@healinglives.com**

You are NOT alone!

_____

_____

_____

_____

_____

The passages on homosexuality are:

Leviticus 18:22

"Do not practice homosexuality, having sex with another man as with a woman. It is a detestable sin (NLT).

Leviticus 20:13

"If a man practices homosexuality, having sex with another man as with a woman, both men have committed a detestable act. They must both be put to death, for they are guilty of a capital offense (NLT).

These two verses clearly condemn homosexuality. What are your reactions to these passages? Questions?

_____

_____

_____

_____

_____

_____

_____

_____

_____

_____

_____

_____

_____

_____

_____

Romans 1:26–27

That is why God abandoned them to their shameful desires. Even the women turned against the natural way to have sex and instead indulged in sex with each other. And the men, instead of having normal sexual relations with women, burned with lust for each other. Men did shameful things with other men, and as a result of this sin, they suffered within themselves the penalty they deserved (NLT).

These verses prohibit same-sex behavior. What is your reaction to this passage?

_____

_____

_____

_____

_____

_____

_____

_____

_____

_____

_____

_____

_____

_____

_____

_____

1 Corinthians 6:9–10

Don't you realize that those who do wrong will not inherit the Kingdom of God? Don't fool yourselves. Those who indulge in sexual sin, or who worship idols, or commit adultery, or are male prostitutes, or practice homosexuality, or are thieves, or greedy people, or drunkards, or are abusive, or cheat people—none of these will inherit the Kingdom of God (NLT).

1 Timothy 1:9–10

For the law was not intended for people who do what is right. It is for people who are lawless and rebellious, who are ungodly and sinful, who consider nothing sacred and defile what is holy, who kill their father or mother or commit other murders. The law is for people who are sexually immoral, or who practice homosexuality, or are slave traders, liars, promise breakers, or who do anything else that contradicts the wholesome teaching (NLT).

These verses mention same-sex sexual behavior. Thoughts? Reactions?

_____

_____

_____

_____

_____

_____

_____

_____

_____

Note here that other sins are listed in some of these lists above — How are you doing in obeying God's Word and staying away from these other sins? None of us are perfect - so which one or one's is your nemesis?

_____

_____

_____

_____

_____

_____

_____

_____

_____

_____

_____

_____

A Biblical Sexual Ethic rests in Scriptures such as these — take notes below each with key highlights, important parts, any questions you may have:

Naked and Unashamed

Explain what these mean to you and how you could use these in conversation with your child.

Genesis 2:24–25

"Therefore a man shall leave his father and his mother and hold fast to his wife, and they shall become one flesh. And the man and his wife were both naked and were not ashamed" (ESV).

_____

_____

_____

_____

_____

_____

_____

_____

_____

_____

_____

_____

_____

Her Breasts

Proverbs 5:18-20

Let your wife be a fountain of blessing for you. Rejoice in the wife of your youth.

She is a loving deer, a graceful doe.

Let her breasts satisfy you always.

May you always be captivated by her love.

Why be captivated, my son, by an immoral woman,

or fondle the breasts of a promiscuous woman? (NLT)

_____

_____

_____

_____

_____

_____

Lust = Adultery

Matthew 5:28

"But I say to you that everyone who looks at a woman with lustful intent has already committed adultery with her in his heart" (ESV).

_____

_____

_____

_____

_____

Become One Flesh

Matthew 19:5

"'Therefore a man shall leave his father and his mother and hold fast to his wife, and the two shall become one flesh'?" (ESV)

_____

_____

_____

_____

_____

_____

_____

Remain Single – Better to Marry than to Burn

1 Corinthians 7:8–9

"To the unmarried and the widows I say that it is good for them to remain single, as I am. But if they cannot exercise self-control, they should marry. For it is better to marry than to burn with passion" (ESV).

_____

_____

_____

_____

_____

_____

_____

Sexual Immorality

Mathew 15:19

"For out of the heart come evil thoughts—murder, adultery, sexual immorality, theft, false testimony, slander" (ESV).

_____

_____

_____

_____

_____

_____

_____

_____

_____

Acts 15:19–20

"Therefore my judgment is that we should not trouble those of the Gentiles who turn to God, but should write to them to abstain from the things polluted by idols, and from sexual immorality...." (ESV).

_____

_____

_____

_____

_____

_____

_____

_____

_____

1 Corinthians 6:18–20

"Flee from sexual immorality. Every other sin a person commits is outside the body, but the sexually immoral person sins against his own body. Or do you not know that your body is a temple of the Holy Spirit within you, whom you have from God? You are not your own, for you were bought with a price. So glorify God in your body" (ESV).

_____

_____

_____

_____

_____

_____

_____

_____

_____

1 Corinthians 7:2–7

"But because of the temptation to sexual immorality, each man should have his own wife and each woman her own husband. The husband should give to his wife her conjugal rights, and likewise the wife to her husband. For the wife does not have authority over her own body, but the husband does. Likewise the husband does not have authority over his own body, but the wife does. Do not deprive one another, except perhaps by agreement for a limited time, that you may devote yourselves to prayer; but then come together

again, so that Satan may not tempt you because of your lack of self-control.

Now as a concession, not a command, I say this. I wish that all were as I myself am. But each has his own gift from God, one of one kind and one of another" (ESV).

_____

_____

_____

_____

_____

_____

_____

_____

Galatians 5:19–21

"Now the works of the flesh are evident: sexual immorality, impurity, sensuality, idolatry, sorcery, enmity, strife, jealousy, fits of anger, rivalries, dissensions, divisions, envy, drunkenness, orgies, and things like these. I warn you, as I warned you before, that those who do such things will not inherit the kingdom of God" (ESV).

_____

_____

_____

_____

_____

_____

_____

_____

Colossians 3:5

"Put to death therefore what is earthly in you: sexual immorality, impurity, passion, evil desire, and covetousness, which is idolatry" (ESV).

_____

_____

_____

_____

_____

_____

_____

_____

1 Thessalonians 4:3–5

"For this is the will of God, your sanctification: that you abstain from sexual immorality; that each one of you know how to control his own body in holiness and honor, not in the passion of lust like the Gentiles who do not know God, not in the passion of lust like the Gentiles who do not know God" (ESV).

_____

_____

_____

_____

_____

_____

_____

_____

Hebrews 13:4

"Let marriage be held in honor among all, and let the marriage bed be undefiled, for God will judge the sexually immoral and adulterous" (ESV).

_____

_____

_____

_____

_____

_____

_____

_____

_____

_____

_____

Same-Sex Attraction

Same-sex attraction might seem like a foreign concept to you. Think about these questions in relation to yourself:

Do you have control of who you are attracted to? Can you see someone and control whether you think they are "good-looking" or not? Do you have the ability NOT to be aroused by someone that you deem attractive? Is arousal sin?

A critical part of attraction is learning to die to some feelings for a certain reason. What are some reasons we deny ourselves things, feelings, attractions, and passions? Why would we ever deny ourselves?

_____

_____

_____

_____

_____

_____

_____

_____

_____

_____

_____

_____

_____

_____

Based off this reading, what should you do if your son or daughter expresses they have attractions toward the same-sex?

_____

_____

_____

_____

_____

_____

_____

What is care and compassion?

_____

_____

_____

_____

_____

_____

_____

_____

_____

CHAPTER 6

YOUR CHILDREN IN TODAY'S WORLD

Pornography

Can you protect your children 100% from pornography?

_____

_____

_____

_____

_____

_____

_____

_____

_____

_____

What are some of the negative effects of viewing pornography?

_____

_____

_____

_____

_____

_____

_____

What is your reaction to learning about the bizarre and troubling types of pornography available such as My Little Pony porn? (I do not advise looking this up.)

_____

_____

_____

_____

_____

_____

_____

_____

Has your child been exposed to pornography? Ask them. If yes, how did you respond? If not, have you had micro-conversations with them about what they should do?

_____

_____

_____

_____

What does "intimacy" mean?

_____
_____
_____
_____
_____
_____
_____
_____

What does "sex over relationship" mean?

_____
_____
_____
_____
_____
_____
_____

What boundaries do you have in place with regards to intimacy, pornography, relationships, and community?

_____
_____
_____
_____
_____
_____
_____
_____

Read Mark 7:20–23

And then he added, "It is what comes from inside that defiles you. For from within, out of a person's heart, come evil thoughts, sexual immorality, theft, murder, adultery, greed, wickedness, deceit, lustful desires, envy, slander, pride, and foolishness. All these vile things come from within; they are what defile you" (NLT).

Explain this passage.

_____

_____

_____

_____

_____

_____

_____

Read **Ephesians 5:3**

Let there be no sexual immorality, impurity, or greed among you. Such sins have no place among God's people (NLT).

Can it be said that there is "not even a hint" of immorality in your own life? How can you teach this with grace to your children?

_____

_____

_____

_____

_____

Write out — **Proverbs 22:6** — again in your favorite translation.

_____

_____

_____

_____

_____

_____

_____

Read **Job 31:1**

"I made a covenant with my eyes

not to look with lust at a young woman (NLT).

Explain how you, your sons or your daughters can live out what Job did. What are some practical ideas?

_____

_____

_____

_____

_____

_____

_____

_____

_____

_____

_____

Read **Proverbs 5:15–23**

Drink water from your own well—

share your love only with your wife.

Why spill the water of your springs in the streets,

having sex with just anyone?

You should reserve it for yourselves.

Never share it with strangers.

Let your wife be a fountain of blessing for you.

Rejoice in the wife of your youth.

She is a loving deer, a graceful doe.

Let her breasts satisfy you always.

May you always be captivated by her love.

Why be captivated, my son, by an immoral woman,

or fondle the breasts of a promiscuous woman?

For the Lord sees clearly what a man does,

examining every path he takes.

An evil man is held captive by his own sins;

they are ropes that catch and hold him.

He will die for lack of self-control;

he will be lost because of his great foolishness. (NLT)

How would you explain this passage to your children? Are you living by this truth?

_____

_____

_____

_____

_____

_____

_____

Read **Proverbs 6:32**

But the man who commits adultery is an utter fool,

for he destroys himself (NLT).

Explain how this destroys him (or her).

_____

_____

_____

_____

_____

_____

_____

_____

_____

_____

_____

Read **Matthew 5:27–28**

"You have heard the commandment that says, 'You must not commit adultery.' But I say, anyone who even looks at a woman with lust has already committed adultery with her in his heart (NLT).

This seems impossible. What are we to learn from this passage? How are you teaching this principle with grace and truth?

_____

_____

_____

_____

_____

_____

Read **Matthew 6:22–23**

"Your eye is like a lamp that provides light for your body. When your eye is healthy, your whole body is filled with light. But when your eye is unhealthy, your whole body is filled with darkness. And if the light you think you have is actually darkness, how deep that darkness is! (NLT)

Explain what this passage teaches. How can we use this in leading and teaching our children?

_____

_____

_____

_____

_____

Read **Romans 13:13–14**

Because we belong to the day, we must live decent lives for all to see. Don't participate in the darkness of wild parties and drunkenness, or in sexual promiscuity and immoral living, or in quarreling and jealousy. Instead, clothe yourself with the presence of the Lord Jesus Christ. And don't let yourself think about ways to indulge your evil desires (NLT).

How can this help in the leading and teaching of our children?

_____

_____

_____

_____

_____

Read **1 Corinthians 6:18–20**

Run from sexual sin! No other sin so clearly affects the body as this one does. For sexual immorality is a sin against your own body. Don't you realize that your body is the temple of the Holy Spirit, who lives in you and was given to you by God? You do not belong to yourself, for God bought you with a high price. So you must honor God with your body (NLT).

Explain what the Lord tells us to do in this passage.

_____

_____

_____

_____

Read **Colossians 3:5**

So put to death the sinful, earthly things lurking within you. Have nothing to do with sexual immorality, impurity, lust, and evil desires. Don't be greedy, for a greedy person is an idolater, worshiping the things of this world (NLT).

How do we "put to death" these things?

_____

_____

_____

_____

_____

_____

_____

_____

Read **1 Thessalonians 4:3–8**

God's will is for you to be holy, so stay away from all sexual sin. Then each of you will control his own body and live in holiness and honor — not in lustful passion like the pagans who do not know God and his ways. Never harm or cheat a fellow believer in this matter by violating his wife, for the Lord avenges all such sins, as we have solemnly warned you before. God has called us to live holy lives, not impure lives. Therefore, anyone who refuses to live by these rules is not disobeying human teaching but is rejecting God, who gives his Holy Spirit to you (NLT).

What does this passage remind us to do and be?

_____

_____

_____

_____

_____

Read **Hebrews 13:4**

Give honor to marriage, and remain faithful to one another in marriage. God will surely judge people who are immoral and those who commit adultery (NLT).

Write out this passage in your own words as a reminder for yourself and to teach your children.

_____

_____

_____

_____

_____

Bullying

Is your son or daughter a bully or being bullied?

_____

_____

_____

_____

_____

_____

Were you bullied as a kid or were you a bully?

_____

_____

_____

_____

_____

Is your son or daughter a leader or a follower?

_____

_____

_____

_____

_____

If they are a leader, are they leading others toward good or astray?

_____

_____

_____

_____

_____

If they are a follower, are there limits to what they would do or where they would go? Do they follow blindly?

_____

_____

_____

_____

_____

_____

What is your goal?

_____

_____

_____

_____

_____

_____

How are you stewarding social media for yourself?

_____

_____

_____

_____

_____

_____

Are you requiring good stewardship of social media for your children? How?

_____

_____

_____

_____

_____

_____

_____

_____

What boundaries and rules do you have in place for smartphones (porn-portal)?

_____

_____

_____

_____

_____

_____

_____

What sorts of issues or problems can arise when children or teenagers have access to a smartphone?

_____

_____

_____

_____

_____

_____

_____

Technology is not evil in and of itself. How can you teach and prepare your children well for this incredible responsibility?

_____

_____

_____

_____

_____

_____

_____

What are your family boundaries and rules for T.V. shows and movies? Does anything need to change on these?

_____

_____

_____

_____

_____

Read **Galatians 5:17**

The sinful nature wants to do evil, which is just the opposite of what the Spirit wants. And the Spirit gives us desires that are the opposite of what the sinful nature desires. These two forces are constantly fighting each other, so you are not free to carry out your good intentions (NLT).

What two forces are mentioned in this passage? Explain these in a way your child could understand.

_____

_____

_____

_____

_____

_____

_____

_____

_____

_____

Influence And Idols

Who are your stars and idols? Who do you admire?
Who do you let entertain you?

_____

_____

_____

_____

_____

How do you talk about celebrities, sports heroes,
singers, and politicians?

_____

_____

_____

_____

_____

When does someone that is famous become an idol,
crossing a line into an unhealthy place?

_____

_____

_____

_____

_____

_____

_____

_____

How does your relationship with the stars and idols impact your children and family, both in time and in money?

_____

_____

_____

_____

_____

_____

Have you intentionally thought through the impact of those relationships on who YOU are, not to mention the impact on your kids and family?

_____

_____

_____

_____

_____

_____

How can you expand or limit (as needed) those influencing your family? What needs to change?

_____

_____

_____

_____

_____

_____

Is there anyone that you should limit your time with because they make you more cynical or depresseed?

_____
_____
_____
_____
_____
_____
_____

Who should you be investing more time with because they are an encouragement and true friend?

_____
_____
_____
_____
_____
_____
_____

Are you a downer to be around and therefore others ought to avoid you? Are you a source of joy, encouragement, and challenge — a true friend?

_____
_____
_____
_____
_____
_____
_____

Can you say, "No," to things, or do you struggle with overcommitting?

_____

_____

_____

_____

_____

_____

_____

Do you live with boundaries? Are they healthy? Unhealthy? Rigid? Flexible? Do you go beyond self-care in putting yourself first? Do others come before you or your family to an unhealthy extent?

_____

_____

_____

_____

_____

_____

_____

_____

_____

_____

_____

Read **Galatians 6:2.** This passage reminds us that we must,

"Share each other's burdens, and in this way obey the law of Christ" (NLT).

Most of us do not know what this actually looks like. We attend church, and we go to this or that event, but in truth we are friendless. Who are other adults speaking into your life and your kids' lives?

_____

_____

_____

_____

_____

_____

_____

_____

_____

_____

_____

_____

_____

Read **Proverbs 18:24**

There are "friends" who destroy each other,

but a real friend sticks closer than a brother (NLT).

Proverbs 17:17

A friend is always loyal,

and a brother is born to help in time of need (NLT).

John 15:13

There is no greater love than to lay down one's life for one's friends (NLT).

Your friends matter. Who are your friends? Name them here. What kind of influence do they have on you?

_____

_____

_____

_____

_____

_____

_____

_____

_____

_____

_____

_____

_____

Read **Philippians 3:7–9**

I once thought these things were valuable, but now I consider them worthless because of what Christ has done. Yes, everything else is worthless when compared with the infinite value of knowing Christ Jesus my Lord. For his sake I have discarded everything else, counting it all as garbage, so that I could gain Christ and become one with him. I no longer count on my own righteousness through obeying the law; rather, I become righteous through faith in Christ. For God's way of making us right with himself depends on faith (NLT).

Are you all in? Have you put your faith in Christ? If not, contact me and let's talk, or go to your church and talk with your pastor or an elder. Make this real in your life! It will change everything.

_____

_____

_____

_____

_____

_____

_____

_____

_____

_____

_____

CHAPTER 7

RAISING SEXUALLY HEALTHY CHILDREN

It Starts With You ~ The Parent

I commit to helping my children develop their OWN ETHOS based on a Biblical Sexual Ethic.

I commit to having micro-conversations—short, meaningful conversations that plant seeds.

I commit to intentionally watering the seeds I have intentionally planted via a carefully chosen community.

I commit to Colossians 3:23 — a stern reminder to: *"Work willingly at whatever you do, as though you were working for the Lord rather than for people" (NLT).*

That is how we must see our work with our children —
as unto the Lord. Do you?

_____

_____

_____

_____

_____

_____

Boundaries And Choices

I commit to the skill of saying, "No."

_____

_____

_____

I have a vision for myself, my family, my children and
their future.

_____

_____

_____

I have hope that my children can be "Champions for
Christ."

_____

_____

_____

_____

Managing Hurts, Failures, And Disappointments

So what is the task for us? First, we must address our story as parents. What are you holding onto? Where are you all tied up by the enemy? Usually this can be found as you review your story. I would dare say that we all have places in our story that need this attention, care, intimacy, and grace.

Is shame ruling how you love or relate to your spouse? Is shame ruling your parenting, or ability to truly love and lead your children?

_____

_____

_____

_____

_____

_____

Do you find yourself honestly hating yourself or others? Does contempt reside in your heart? Gratitude and contempt cannot coexist in the same heart.

_____

_____

_____

_____

_____

Do you find yourself putting on a mask and being fake around others? Are you unable to be honest with those close to you?

_____

_____

_____

_____

_____

Do you have areas in your story where you still need to forgive and let go?

_____

_____

_____

_____

_____

I commit to growth and JOY!

Read **Proverbs 31:25**

She is clothed with strength and dignity,

and she laughs without fear of the future (NLT).

This passage refers to strength, dignity, and laughter for tomorrow. What do these mean?

_____

_____

_____

_____

_____

Read **Philippians 4:7**

Then you will experience God's peace, which exceeds anything we can understand. His peace will guard your hearts and minds as you live in Christ Jesus (NLT).

Do you have that peace?

_____

_____

_____

_____

_____

_____

_____

_____

_____

_____

CHAPTER 8

DATING, THE "M" WORD, AND TRAUMA

Singleness, Sexuality, And Dating

Your teenager thinks they are ready to date. Are they prepared to steward that kind of responsibility?

_____

_____

_____

_____

_____

_____

_____

Your twenty-one year old is sexually active, but not married. How can you come alongside them and share

_____

_____

_____

_____

_____

_____

_____

_____

Define dating.

_____

_____

_____

_____

Define courtship.

_____

_____

_____

_____

_____

How do you teach your child to have an ETHOS and morals that lead them to wise decisions in their adolescent years and young adult years?

_____

_____

_____

_____

_____

_____

Describe the Relationship Continuum with all seven words.

_____

_____

_____

_____

_____

_____

_____

_____

_____

_____

Decide now whether you are going to play Russian roulette with your children's genitals bringing babies into this world prematurely, or contracting and spreading sexually transmitted infections — many that are fatal.

The "M" Word

What approach will you take in discussing masturbation with your children?

_____

_____

_____

_____

_____

_____

Will you take the medical approach, the stereotypical punitive church approach, or another one?

_____

_____

_____

_____

_____

_____

How can these micro-conversations be redemptive instead of shameful and punitive?

_____

_____

_____

_____

_____

_____

_____

Addressing Past Trauma

When your child leaves home and goes to preschool, are they prepared? For everything? When your child joins a sports team, are they prepared?

_____

_____

_____

_____

_____

_____

Fight, flight, and _____? Explain how each of these can be a response to trauma.

_____

_____

_____

_____

_____

_____

What is building resilience?

_____

_____

_____

_____

_____

_____

From birth to five our children are absorbing our family's
_____. Explain.

_____

_____

_____

_____

_____

_____

Between ages six and ten our children are absorbing
our family's _____. Explain.

_____

_____

_____

_____

_____

_____

Between the ages of eleven to seventeen our children
are entering the peak of their sexual interest and
curiosity — have you prepared them? Are you going to
now? Do you have a plan?

_____

_____

_____

_____

_____

_____

CHAPTER 9

BUILDING YOUR PERSONAL ETHOS

Building My Personal Ethos

Define ETHOS.

_____

_____

_____

_____

_____

_____

_____

_____

_____

_____

As you process all we have covered, what are some areas that are painful for you to remember or realize about your parenting?

_____

_____

_____

_____

_____

_____

_____

What are some questions that emerge?

_____

_____

_____

_____

_____

_____

Can you see clearly a path for them that has the least amount of pain and is full of joy, strong relationships, strength of character, and success? What does that path look like?

_____

_____

_____

_____

_____

_____

Spend some time writing out a list of areas you fear discussing with your children.

_____

_____

_____

_____

_____

_____

_____

Why is it so important for us to "go there?"

_____

_____

_____

_____

_____

_____

_____

Your Living ETHOS — Give some more detail about what you want them to do in this space:

Gender

_____

_____

_____

_____

_____

_____

Pornography

_____

_____

_____

_____

_____

_____

Dating

_____

_____

_____

_____

_____

Marriage

_____

_____

_____

Sex

_____

_____

_____

_____

_____

Technology

_____
_____
_____
_____
_____
_____
_____

Idols

_____
_____
_____
_____
_____
_____

Now it is your turn to make this YOURS. The next steps may involve research, prayer, and getting on the same page as your spouse, if you are a couple, is crucial so that you can lead with intentionality, integrity, and with a realistic and biblical picture of what could be.

Proverbs 27:17 says that

As iron sharpens iron,

so a friend sharpens a friend (NLT).

It is in the fellowship with others that we grow.

_____

_____

_____

_____

_____

_____

Look this one up:

We are to "... be happy in your _____"
(**Ecclesiastes 3:22**). Are you?

_____

_____

_____

Read **Genesis 1:15–24**

_Let these lights in the sky shine down on the earth." And
that is what happened. God made two great lights—
the larger one to govern the day, and the smaller one
to govern the night. He also made the stars. God set
these lights in the sky to light the earth, to govern
the day and night, and to separate the light from the
darkness. And God saw that it was good._

_And evening passed and morning came, marking the
fourth day._

_Then God said, "Let the waters swarm with fish and
other life. Let the skies be filled with birds of every
kind." So God created great sea creatures and every
living thing that scurries and swarms in the water, and
every sort of bird—each producing offspring of the_

same kind. And God saw that it was good. Then God blessed them, saying, "Be fruitful and multiply. Let the fish fill the seas, and let the birds multiply on the earth."

And evening passed and morning came, marking the fifth day.

Then God said, "Let the earth produce every sort of animal, each producing offspring of the same kind— livestock, small animals that scurry along the ground, and wild animals." And that is what happened (NLT).

Verses 27-28:

So God created human beings in his own image.

In the image of God he created them;

male and female he created them.

Then God blessed them and said, "Be fruitful and multiply. Fill the earth and govern it. Reign over the fish in the sea, the birds in the sky, and all the animals that scurry along the ground" (NLT).

This passage reminds us of God's perfect design. What is this design for marriage and children?

_____

_____

_____

_____

_____

_____

I Have A Plan
My Theology Of Sex

Write out Scripture and other ideas and resources that help inform your ETHOS on sex.

_____
_____
_____
_____
_____
_____
_____

Why should I wait until marriage to have genital contact with another person?

_____
_____
_____
_____
_____
_____

What is your response to this question from your child? What is the harm in sexual play?

_____
_____
_____
_____

What is my theology of oral sex? Everyone seems to say it is okay, but is it really? Is it healthy or unhealthy? Is it harmful? Sick? Gross? Is it another acceptable part of healthy sexual play within marriage?

_____

_____

_____

_____

_____

_____

_____

Is it okay to have a third person in the sexual relationship? Why not?

_____

_____

_____

_____

_____

_____

_____

What do I do with my sex drive as a single adult with raging hormones? This feels like a cruel punishment from God.

_____

_____

_____

_____

What do I desire in a healthy sexual relationship in marriage one day? If I desire my spouse to be pure, what am I doing to keep the same commitment?

_____
_____
_____
_____
_____
_____
_____
_____
_____

Do you have more questions? Write them here. Wrestle with them as you seek an answer in Scripture and seek wise counsel.

_____
_____
_____
_____
_____
_____
_____
_____
_____
_____
_____

My Theology Of Marriage

What is your theology of marriage? Write out the beliefs you have about marriage — whether they are crazy, funny, wild, anything! Ponder on your beliefs. Are they biblical? Do they line up with what God's Word says?

_____

_____

_____

_____

_____

_____

Am I teaching my theology of marriage to my children? Is it biblical or just wishful thinking?

_____

_____

_____

_____

_____

_____

Am I cynical and I need to lighten up or am I a hopeless romantic and I need to wise up?

_____

_____

_____

_____

Should a believer marry an unbeliever? How would you advise your children?

_____
_____
_____
_____
_____
_____
_____

Is marriage designed to be only between a man and woman? How would you teach this to your children? Does the Word of God inform your beliefs here — or popular culture?

_____
_____
_____
_____
_____
_____
_____

Are there requirements for marriage? Does Scripture have some I can glean?

_____
_____
_____
_____
_____

What does it mean to be "sexually compatiable"? Is this important? How do you know?

_____

_____

_____

_____

_____

_____

Do you believe that the Lord would call a couple in two different directions? What should you do if you believe you are being led down different paths?

_____

_____

_____

_____

_____

_____

Is friendship a foundation for a great marriage? If we do not have that, can we ever find it?

_____

_____

_____

_____

_____

What role does forgiveness play in marriage?

_____
_____
_____
_____
_____
_____
_____

What are some other questions that come to mind as you think about your marriage? Your story? What are your fears, hang ups, and struggles? What comes to mind as you think about your children, their future, their future spouses?

_____
_____
_____
_____
_____
_____
_____
_____
_____
_____
_____
_____
_____

I Commit To Living By A Plan

I lead by _____. Explain.

_____

_____

_____

_____

_____

_____

_____

_____

I lead with _____. Explain.

_____

_____

_____

_____

_____

_____

_____

_____

I lead with _____. Explain.

_____

_____

_____

_____

_____

CHAPTER 10

THE POWER AND IMPORTANCE OF COMMUNITY

Reminders And Challenges

Your children are gifts from God. How are you stewarding these gifts that He has left in your care, dependent on you for their future selves?

_____

_____

_____

_____

_____

_____

Do you feel like you have failed your children? There is always hope. Even parents that might get this part right will miss other things their children need. What are areas beyond sexuality that need your attention and investment?

_____

_____

_____

_____

_____

_____

_____

_____

_____

Have you prepared them for that, whatever that is?

_____

_____

_____

_____

_____

_____

_____

_____

_____

_____

_____

_____

id you discuss stranger danger and prepare them
r the nine percent chance of abuse from a stranger,
ut never prepare them to say no and stand up for
emselves when a sibling, uncle, or family friend asks
em to take their clothes off or do something sexual?

_____

_____

_____

_____

_____

_____

_____

_____

_____

_____

hy is this important? Be an example of someone
at is teachable. Honestly, your child can easily look
ything up online, as scary as that is. Invite them to
me to you. Do life together in relationship with them.
 huge part of this confidence is humility. Are you
nfident? Are you humble?

_____

_____

_____

_____

_____

_____

_____

Write **Proverbs 22:6** out again as a reminder.

_____

_____

_____

_____

Write out **John 15:13**

Are you doing this for your children? Friends? Family?
How does this verse impact you?

_____

_____

_____

_____

_____

_____

_____

_____

Community

Who is in your community?

_____

_____

_____

_____

_____

Who can you call at a moment's notice for help, to talk, to cry, to vent—or to go to a movie, laugh with, and spend quality time with?

_____

_____

_____

_____

_____

_____

_____

Who, outside of your family, do you spend the most time with? What are those people's beliefs and values? Do you want to be like them? Do you want your children to be like them?

_____

_____

_____

_____

_____

_____

_____

How are you SEEKING community in your life—for your family, for your children, for yourself?

_____

_____

_____

_____

_____

How are you BEING community for others?

_____

_____

_____

_____

_____

_____

_____

_____

_____

_____

Write out Galatians 6:2 as a reminder.

_____

_____

_____

_____

_____

_____

_____

_____

What's Next?

Marriage and Family Life Coaching and Counseling services are available at

www.HealingLives.com

Access more resources including video trainings and more content for free at

parentbook.healinglives.com

For further in depth training as a parent or as a leader find out more about further resouces at:

www.HealingLives.com

Reach out to someone and get help, aid, new learning, be challenged — we are always in process. Be teachable. Will you find help, as needed?

Your final assignment: get the support you need — somewhere.

Bless you and your family legacy.

Dr. Gilbert

CPSIA information can be obtained
at www.ICGtesting.com
Printed in the USA
LVHW041316310822
727261LV00010B/730